Farewell t

Richard Nelson's plays include *Farewell to the Theatre*, *Nikolai and the Others*, *Sweet and Sad*, *That Hopey Changey Thing*, *Conversations in Tusculum*, *How Shakespeare Won the West*, *Frank's Home*, *Rodney's Wife*, *Franny's Way*, *Madame Melville*, *Goodnight Children Everywhere*, *The General From America*, *New England*, *Misha's Party* (with Alexander Gelman), *Columbus or the Discovery of Japan*, *Two Shakespearean Actors*, *Some Americans Abroad*, *Left*, *Life Sentences* and *Principia Scriptoriae*. He has written the musicals *Unfinished Piece for a Player Piano* (with Peter Golub); *James Joyce's The Dead* (with Shaun Davey), *My Life with Albertine* (with Ricky Ian Gordon); and screenplays for the films *Hyde Park-on-Hudson* (Roger Michell director) and *Ethan Frome* (John Madden director).

He has received numerous awards both in America and abroad, including a Tony Award (Best Book of a Musical for *James Joyce's The Dead*), an Olivier Award (Best Play for *Goodnight Children Everywhere*), Tony nominations (Best Play for *Two Shakespearean Actors*; Best Score as co-lyricist for *James Joyce's The Dead*), an Olivier nomination (Best Comedy for *Some Americans Abroad*), two Obies, a Lortel Award, a New York Drama Critics' Circle Award, a Guggenheim Fellowship and a Lila Wallace–Reader's Digest Writers Award. He is recipient of the PEN/Laura Pels Master Playwright Award, an Academy Award from the American Academy of Arts and Letters, and is an Honorary Associate Artist of the Royal Shakespeare Company. He lives in upstate New York.

RICHARD NELSON

Farewell to the Theatre

faber and faber

First published in 2012
by Faber and Faber Limited
74–77 Great Russell Street, London WC1B 3DA

Typeset by Country Setting, Kingsdown, Kent CT14 8ES
Printed in England by CPI Group (UK) Ltd, Croydon CR0 4YY

A CIP record for this book
is available from the British Library

ISBN 978-0-571-28073-5

FSC
www.fsc.org
MIX
Paper from
responsible sources
FSC® C101712

2 4 6 8 10 9 7 5 3 1

To Roger Michell

Farewell to the Theatre was first performed at the Hampstead Theatre, London, on 1 March 2012. The cast was as follows:

Harley Ben Chaplin
Dorothy Jemma Redgrave
Henry Louis Hilyer
George Andrew Havill
Beatrice Tara Fitzgerald
Frank Jason Watkins
Charles William French

Director Roger Michell
Designer Hildegard Bechtler
Lighting Designer Rick Fisher
Sound Designer John Leonard

Characters

Harley Granville Barker
thirty-nine,
playwright, director, producer, lecturer

Frank Spraight
forty-five, Dickens recitalist

Charles Massinger
twenty, American, student, Williams College

Dorothy Blackwell
thirty-seven, widow,
manageress of the boarding house

Henry Smith
thirty-nine, Dorothy's brother,
associate professor, Williams College

George Scully
thirty-five, Henry and Dorothy's cousin,
teacher in a boys' school

Beatrice Hale
thirty-five, actress, lecturer

All of the characters are English except for Charles

A day in April 1916, in and around a boarding house
in Williamstown, Massachusetts. And weeks later.

FAREWELL TO THE THEATRE

'I must pray now to the moon . . .
as one burnt-out lady to another'

Joan Westerbury, in
Harley Granville Barker's *The Secret Life*

Williamstown, Massachusetts.

   The back lawn of a boarding house (Mrs Dorothy Blackwell, manageress), near the college campus.

   Outdoor chairs. Late morning.

   Harley sits talking with Charles, twenty, American, a student at Williams College. Harley has been opening his accumulated post; he holds a small pile of opened and unopened letters and a letter opener. He has been interrupted by Charles, whom he has just met. Frank, forty-five, English, sits apart, reading the college newspaper.

   It is a grey though warm April day.

Harley So my wife –

Charles I think Miss McCarthy is extraordinary.

Harley (*surprised*) Thank you. (*Beat.*) She is. In many ways. (*To himself.*) In more ways than you can imagine . . . She'd be happy to know that – that the young men still – (*Gestures to Charles.*)

Charles I thought her Hermia was great.

Harley You saw that?

Charles Everyone did. The entire Cap and Bells went to New York to see *Midsummer*.

Harley (*figuring something out*) So – some of those students – had they actually seen my work?

Charles Most of them. Yes. (*Beat.*) And the Greek plays too. We all went to New Haven to see them. Why are you surprised?

3

Harley No one seemed to . . . You all looked – blank. When I was talking. But perhaps not. (*Shrugs. To Frank.*) Perhaps they understood more than I thought, Frank. Perhaps I shouldn't have complained . . .

Frank (*head in his paper*) Students always look blank when I talk to them too. You get used to that.

Charles What did you complain about?

Harley (*to Charles*) So you understood some of what I was saying? *Some* of you did. In my talk?

Charles Of course.

Harley Good. That's – good. (*To Frank.*) I couldn't tell.

Charles (*back to the earlier subject*) You were saying something about Miss McCarthy . . .

Harley I was saying that – (*smiles*) for one production. In fact, for *that Midsummer* actually – we need to raise money. (*To Frank.*) She's brilliant at that. Getting people to give her things. It's a gift. (*To Charles.*) She met this Lord. Who owned a pig farm. And somehow she got him to sell the pigs, and give us the money to put on Shakespeare.

Looks at Frank, incredulous.

It's true. From pigs to Shakespeare! (*To Charles.*) And that's how theatre is made now. At least in London. (*To Frank.*) And there are just so many pigs. (*Looks at Charles.*) You don't understand.

Frank has found the story very funny.

Have you two met? I'm sorry. (*Gestures to Frank.*) Frank, this is Charles – he's the President of Cap and Bells.

Charles How did you know that? That just happened yesterday –

4

Harley I have my ear to the ground, my boy. And – he's our Feste for tonight.

Frank The *Twelfth Night*?

Harley Mr Spraight. Mr Massinger.

Charles and Frank shake hands.

Charles How do you do?

Harley Mr Spraight only just arrived last night. (*To Frank.*) I didn't tell you – I saw an *all-girl Twelfth Night* at Holyoke the other day? It was – (*looks for the word*) memorable. (*Smiles.*) The Sir Toby will not soon be forgotten. To tell you the truth, I enjoyed myself. (*To Charles.*) As I'm sure I will enjoy tonight.

Charles Are you also in the theatre, Mr Spraight?

Harley (*before Frank can ans*wer) Mr Spraight is the Dickens man. You don't recognise him?

Frank Harley –

Harley I'm serious. Frank Spraight is an important man.

Charles I don't know you. I'm sorry. I'm sure I should.

Harley (*to Frank*) Where's that clipping you were showing me?

Frank Please, Harley. He's not interested –

Harley Give it to me. He should be. He should know who you are.

Frank Are you making fun of me?

Harley I am not. Give it to me.

Harley has stood up and Frank hands him a newspaper clipping he had in his pocket.

Frank Don't read it out loud.

Harley (*reads*) 'Frank Spraight, who has obtained a high reputation in England for his interpretations of Dickens's novels, gave a reading from *Pickwick Papers* at the Hudson Theatre yesterday afternoon . . . The accuracy and certainty with which he repeated the text of seven chapters –' (*repeats for effect*) 'seven chapters – was an unusual feat in memorising.' (*As he hands back the clipping, to Charles.*) *New York Times.*

Frank We all have to make a living, Harley. Don't make fun. He can be very mean, Mr Massinger. He has a mean tongue.

Charles What are you doing at Williams College, sir?

Harley He's doing *Pickwick*, aren't you? This afternoon? At a fraternity house, correct?

Frank I do it wherever they pay me. (*To Charles.*) I think some parents are visiting and so the boys wanted to impress them.

Harley I wasn't making fun –

Frank You can come if you'd like, Harley. (*To Charles.*) You too.

No response.

(*As he puts away the clipping, to Harley.*) What I *didn't* tell you is that the writer –

Holds up the clipping of the article.

– had a copy of the book with him. And followed along. That was nerve-racking.

Puts the clipping away in his pocket.

Harley We – English. We come here and we trade Dickens, Shakespeare – for what? Animal pelts!

Frank (*smiling at the joke*) Harley . . .

Charles I don't understand.

Harley Forgive me, Charles. I am being . . . silly. (*To Frank.*) And I wasn't making fun – And I am not mean. In the American sense, that is.

   Frank has gone back to his paper.
   George, thirty-five, enters from the house.

George Why isn't there any tea?

Harley Out here in the wilds? Should there be?

George I'll bring the urn out.

   He starts to go back.

Harley George – Have you met Mr Massinger?

George Many times. Hello, Charles. I'll be right back. With tea.

   He goes.

Frank (*head in paper, calls*) Could you bring cups?! (*To no one.*) You think he heard me?

   Short pause.

Harley (*to Frank, about George*) Do you know Scully?

Frank I do.

   Smiles, then goes back to reading the paper.
   Harley turns to Charles.

Harley So – Charles – what can I do for you? What do you want?

Charles What do I want? I don't want anything.

Harley I don't understand. Then why are you here?

Charles (*realises*) I didn't come to see you, Mr Barker. I just recognised, so . . . I'm meeting Mrs Hale. She's a guest too. She arrived last night?

Harley (*to Frank*) Mrs Hale?

Frank Beatrice? She arrived with me. We were on the same train.

Harley (*smiling to Charles*) I thought you were here to see me. (*To Frank.*) I know Beatrice. (*As a joke, to Charles.*) So why am I talking to you? That is a joke. (*Beat.*) I look forward to your play tonight. One of my favourite plays. I've even directed it.

Charles We're all nervous that you're coming, Mr Barker.

Harley You should be. (*Smiles.*) That is a joke.

He goes back to opening his letters.

(*To Frank.*) I didn't tell you that Scully has been following me around all month. First to Wellesley. Then Amherst. He's got a talk.

Frank I didn't know he did that. He teaches young boys . . .

Harley He's making money off the tercentenary.

Charles What's that?

Harley Of Shakespeare's death. We all hope to live off that for a while. (*To Frank.*) So he has this talk – 'Education in the Time of Shakespeare'. As illustrated by the schoolbooks which Shakespeare probably used.

Frank How does he know –?

Harley He doesn't. But he has a suitcase full of old-looking books, that he passes around. A friend told me that one of them is about eight years old.

Smiles. He is looking at a letter. Folds it back up.

Charles He's given that talk here.

Harley Has he?

Charles It was popular.

George comes out carrying a large hot water urn and a small table. Dorothy, the manageress, thirty-seven, follows with a tray of cups, the tea, etc. She is dressed in black.

Dorothy It's not going to rain?

She is ignored.
Harley has opened a letter and reads.

Harley (*to Frank*) A friend writes that Shaw was heard saying that he hoped the next bomb to hit London would land on Parliament.

Frank Does anyone even listen to Shaw any more? Isn't he a crackpot now?

George Frank, show Harley your clipping. He showed me last night.

Harley I've seen it.

He looks at Frank.

George I have to use notes for my talk. I wish I had his memory.

Frank It's a curse. I can't forget anything!

They laugh.
Harley looks at another unopened letter. Frank sees the expression on his face.

Lillah?

Harley nods. and sets the letter aside, to open later.

Harley (*picking up another letter, to Frank*) My wife had a friend write to me last week saying she was now ready to play Lady Macbeth. When will I arrange that?

Charles I'd love to see that.

Harley (*to himself*) I *think* he meant in a theatre . . . (*To Charles.*) Well, you won't. (*To Frank.*) Her friend says, she'll even stoop to play it in America. Because there's money here. (*Then to himself as he looks on the ground.*) Where? (*Folds up the letter.*) She couldn't write herself?

Frank I thought – she just did.

Gestures to the unopened letter.

Harley (*changing the subject, opening another letter*) Where's your brother, Mrs Blackwell? I haven't seen him this morning.

Dorothy He's already teaching. He has a class.

Harley (*to Charles*) Why aren't you in class?

Charles It's Saturday. And I've already had French.

George We used to have classes all day on Saturday.

Harley (*looking at a letter*) At acting school we did two performances every Saturday.

Charles I'm doing a show . . .

Beatrice Hale, thirty-five, English, has arrived from the house. and stops the conversation.

Beatrice It feels like it's going to rain.

Dorothy That's what I told them.

Harley looks up at Beatrice, smiles politely and goes back to the letter.

Harley (*about the letter, to Frank*) The publishers like my Red Cross book . . .

Beatrice What is that?

Frank Harley was just in France. Writing a book.

Beatrice France must be awful now.

Frank (*explaining the book, to Beatrice and the others*) This to avoid being a soldier.

Harley (*still with the note*) There's no conscription for married men yet. So there's nothing to avoid. Yet. Yes, France *is* awful.

Dorothy is setting up the tea urn.

Beatrice Mr Barker, I had no idea you were here as well. Mrs Blackwell only told me last night. When we got in. (*Nods to Frank.*) Frank.

George (*at the urn*) Who's having tea?

Beatrice (*greeting him*) Charles . . .

She shakes his hand.

(*To Harley.*) You've met?

Harley Charles was at my lecture. He found it very interesting. He's seen everything I have ever done.

Charles (*confused*) That's not true.

Harley I wasn't interesting?

Charles (*flustered*) I didn't –

Frank (*to Charles*) He doesn't mean . . . Ignore him, old chap.

Beatrice (*to Charles*) What did you see of Mr Barker's?

Harley My *Midsummer*.

Beatrice With the gold? I saw that.

George is passing out cups of tea.

George What gold?

Beatrice Everything. Even some of the actors' beards. Correct?

Harley (*beginning a list*) The fairies –

Beatrice I have a girlfriend who knew someone who was – I don't know who. I asked her how they did it, she said – it was all paint.

Harley True. Gold leaf.

Beatrice (*over this*) Gold leaf. Head to toe.

Harley Thirty-five cents a fairy. Every performance.

Frank My God . . .

Harley So I wouldn't let them – the fairies – wash it off between matinee and evening shows.

Beatrice So they couldn't go out?

Harley Oh, they went out. They just went out gold.

Dorothy (*having finished with the urn*) George, there are little cakes inside.

George It's going to rain.

Dorothy Please, George.

She heads off.

George No one wants a cake, do they?

Frank I would. I would like one.

Harley Why not? Mrs Hale?

George (*heading inside*) Don't tell any good stories without me.

Beatrice (*about George*) He's not a guest?

Harley The cousin. He seems to come all the time. (*Explaining the letters.*) Two weeks' worth. They appear to deliver once every two weeks here.

Frank There's a war –

Harley I know there's a war.

Beatrice How long have you been here?

Harley (*hesitates, then*) A month. A little more.

Beatrice And lecturing. I hear.

Harley Yes. (*Then, from his lecture.*) 'Today the theatre has failed all of us, and we suffer from this failure.' (*To Charles.*) Do you remember that, young Mr Charles? Were you one of the few awake?

> *Charles doesn't know what to say.*

I suppose he wasn't.

Beatrice How's Lillah?

> *Short pause.*

Harley In England. Acting. (*Beat.*) Performing. Every hour of every day.

Beatrice Safer to be here.

Harley That is true.

> *Short pause. They sip their tea.*
> *Beatrice smiles at Charles.*

Beatrice (*explaining*) Charles and I haven't seen each other for months . . .

> *She smiles at him again, takes his hand and pats it, then realises others are watching.*

His father couldn't come to see the play. Charles's father and my husband are law partners. That's how we . . . I've known Charles for a long time. Haven't I?

Smiles again at him.

Charles Yes.

Others watch this. Awkward pause.

Harley Charles is the new head of the Drama Society.

Beatrice Are you? When did that happen? You didn't tell me –

Charles Yesterday.

Beatrice That's wonderful. You wanted that, didn't you?

He nods. She looks at him.

Harley George and I saw him in a Smoker a couple of weeks ago.

Beatrice What's that?

Harley A kind of men's party – with a show. And cigars. Hence . . . Charles was – the Queen of Sheba?

Charles Siam. Queen of Siam.

Harley Sat on a throne and everything. Has a nice singing voice.

Charles Thank you.

Harley They wrote the songs themselves.

Beatrice (*to Charles*) You didn't invite me.

Charles Women can't come.

Pause. They sip their tea. Maybe Harley looks at another letter.

Beatrice Frank?

She looks to Frank, and then to Charles. Frank gets up.

Frank (*to Charles*) Come with me . . . Come on.

Charles (*to Beatrice*) What am I doing?

Beatrice Go with Frank. He'll explain.

Charles (*as they go*) You'll explain what?

Frank leads Charles off towards the house. Harley watches.

Harley Where are they going?

Beatrice ignores the question.

Beatrice Frank and I were on the same train.

Harley He said.

Beatrice suddenly stands and 'stretches'.

Frank is doing his *Pickwick* this afternoon. If you're free . . .

Beatrice I'm not.

Looks at him, and after a glance towards the house.

This is a little embarrassing. As I said, I didn't know someone I knew would be here.

Harley He got a very nice notice for his *Pickwick* –

Beatrice Frank's room. It's on the far side of the house. It's more private than mine. Mine is – next to Mrs Blackwell's. So . . . All the other rooms in town – there are a lot of parties this weekend.

Harley I heard.

Beatrice A lot of young women. Charles lives in a dorm.

Short pause.

Harley How are the children?

Beatrice Fine.

Beat.

Where is he? They must have run into her . . . My God, what you must think?

Harley I don't think anything any more.

Beatrice My husband doesn't know. Of course. (*She looks at him. Then:*) The train last night seemed to take for ever.

Harley It can sometimes. When you want to get somewhere.

Beatrice (*suddenly a change of subject*) And what are you doing here, Harley? What are you doing in – of all inappropriate places – Williamstown?

Harley Lecturing. Trying to write. Waiting for Lillah to divorce me.

This surprises her.

Which I hope she'll do very soon.

Beatrice When did that . . .? I'm sorry. Is there someone else?

Harley There is.

Beatrice I'm sorry.

Harley Someone else for me, not for her. At least not that I know of.

She thinks about this.

Beatrice How has Lillah taken the news?

Harley She's a wee bit upset with me. (*Then:*) Let's just say she doesn't seem to tire of telling our friends what sort of person I am. How they must never – or God help them – speak to me again. That keeps her busy. Seems to be taking up the bulk of her time. We shared a lot of friends.

Beat.

Helen is here.

Beatrice 'Helen' . . . ?

Harley I mean – in America.

Frank returns.

She's American. But we have to – stay apart. Propriety.

Frank hands Beatrice the key to his room.

We write.

She looks at Harley, but has nothing to say, and hurries off. Frank sits back down and picks up his paper.

Frank She said she'd pay for my room. All of it. I need the money.

Short pause.

Harley Her uncle's a friend. More than a friend. He's a hero of mind. Forbes-Robertson.

Frank She's his niece?

Harley He asked me when I first came over –

Frank I loved his Hamlet.

Harley So did I. – To see how she was. She is married to this man . . . I remember him saying – (*smiles*) that the law was theatre. And he – as a lawyer – was the playwright. And sometimes – the actor. And sometimes – the audience. I asked him if he ever sat in the cheap seats. He didn't understand. Crude, crude man. I loathed him. She loathed him already. I begged her to go back.

Frank Why didn't she?

Harley Why doesn't anyone? Why didn't you? (*Beat.*) She had the excuse of being pregnant. Already had one child. I heard then it was twins. So she was stuck. Marooned. (*Looks to Frank.*) She couldn't go back. No, now she was – an American. At least she seems to be making the most of that now.

Frank She says she still wants to act. And she lectures. Women's schools.

George returns.

George (*hesitates, then*) I have to do errands in town. Where did they go?

Frank For a walk.

He looks back into his paper.

Harley Where are the little cakes?

George I forgot. She gave me a list of things to get and – Do you really want cakes?

No response.

It's going to rain anyway. Anyone want to come with me?

No response. Frank reads the paper, Harley opens another letter.

Anyone need anything?

He pours more tea for himself and sits and sips it. Frank looks at him, surprised to see him sitting down.

The town is going to be crowded. A lot of the fraternities are having their parties this weekend.

Frank (*as he reads*) Our train was packed with young ladies.

Looks up to George.

Where do they all stay? They must pack them in five, ten to a room.

George The Williams Inn is full, I know. My cousin got telephone calls – looking for rooms. She wanted to rent mine. (*He laughs.*) She said she was joking.

He hesitates while the others read.

Are you going to any of the parties?

Harley He's doing his *Pickwick* at one.

George Of course.
   When I was a student, I loved weekends like this. Winter's over. Flowers coming out – girls arriving. (*Smiles.*) I love it here. I wish I lived here . . . Do you think it's going to rain?

Harley (*reading*) I don't know.

George It smells so good here when it rains.

Dorothy (*off*) George! My shopping!

George (*calls*) I'm going!!

He doesn't get up. Suddenly the bell of the college chapel rings. George listens.

I love that. Makes you feel like you're in some Renaissance world. Doesn't it?

Frank (*without looking up*) I'm in western Massachusetts.

George (*smiles, then*) When I was in university – years and years ago – (*Laughs to himself.*) On one weekend like this – when we all had girls and there were parties. Once my cousin was my 'girl'. That was a bad idea.

We had what you could only call – (*smiling*) a singing contest. Between the classes. In the gymnasium. We'd line up, the different classes, grouped together, on one side, and on the other, across the gymnasium, against the wall – our ladies. The point was to sing the loudest. To the ladies. Actually, at them.

He laughs at the memory. The others are listening to him now.

Shout, really. Songs we'd written. Someone had. I hadn't. Someone with real talent.

And so we'd be shouting and singing and the ladies would be cheering, screaming . . . my God . . . I remember our faces – beetroot red. And their feet, someone told me to look at their feet – blushing. I'd never seen anything like it. (*Then to Harley.*) You're a writer. You should write about a place like this.

Harley goes back to his letters.

(*To Frank*) Maybe he already is. I see him sitting out here writing.

Dorothy (*off*) George!

George I'm going. I'm going . . . (*Finishes his tea, stands up.*) I should never have brought a cousin . . . (*Beat.*) Girls there, boys there . . .

Shakes his head at the memory.
  He heads off to town.
  Harley sits up and looks towards the house.

Frank He teaches ten-year-olds in a school in Connecticut. What are you doing?

Harley Wondering which window is yours.

Frank Henry was telling me –

Harley When did you talk to Henry? You just arrived.

Frank This morning. Before you got up.

Harley Don't you sleep?

Frank No. I don't sleep. And I don't forget. A lethal combination. Henry was saying that George thinks he's going to get offered a job here. At the college. That's why he keeps coming back. To make an impression.

Harley Are there jobs here?

Frank In the English Department, with Henry. George had heard a rumour . . . So now they can't get rid of him. He pestered Henry until they let him give his lecture about the books young Shakespeare might have read . . . (*Smiles.*)

Harley What sort of job? A professor?

Frank I suppose. I don't know. Why do you care?

Harley shrugs and goes back to his letters.

You wouldn't want to teach here.

Harley I am broke. I have to do something.
Seems like a nice life. Read books. Relax. Students look up to you. Something tells me Lillah is not about to send me money . . .

Frank And – Helen?

Harley Rich husband. He's a wee bit upset with her as well.

Frank Have you talked to Henry about this?

Harley (*opening a letter*) Henry seems scared of me for some reason. We've hardly said two words to each other all month.

Frank I think Henry's just scared.

Harley Perhaps you're right. (*Feeling the rain.*) Has it started to rain?

He starts to stand up.

Frank (*reading the paper*) A little drizzle. Like home. (*Reads.*) 'Charles Massinger new Cap and Bell head.'

Harley sits back down. Frank holds up the paper to show Harley.

(*Reads.*) 'Charles Jerome Massinger, class of 'seventeen, was elected President at a meeting yesterday afternoon in Jessup Hall.'

Harley (*saluting towards the house*) Congratulations, Charles Jerome Massinger!

They laugh. Harley picks up the letter from Lillah that he has set aside. Frank notices this.

(*Explaining.*) I have to read it sometime . . .

Frank folds the paper.

Frank I should warm up. Do you mind?

As Harley reads his letter.

It's hardly raining.
My wife says I speak Dickens in my sleep. Sometimes, when she was in the mood, she said, she'd listen to a whole chapter before poking me. (*Smiles.*)

Harley folds Lillah's letter and puts it back in the envelope.

Harley How is your wife, Frank?

Frank Good days, bad days.

He stands, limbers up.

So – you're writing. George said he saw you writing.

Harley A play. (*Beat.*) It's not raining, is it?

Frank shrugs and limbers up.

(*Continuing.*) About an actress who abandons the theatre. Chucks it all because – (*Shrugs.*) It's not what she wants. It's become – suffocating. A business . . . Nothing to be proud of. So she chucks it.

Frank Henry's used to me. He's over being scared of me. I'll talk to him . . .

Harley I don't know what I want . . .

He sits back lost in thought, pulling up his collar because of the rain.
Frank clears his throat, and then to himself, doing dramatically different voices, recites:

Frank ' "How old is that horse, my friend?' inquired Mr Pickwick, rubbing his nose with the shilling he had reserved for the fare.
"Forty-two," replied the driver, eyeing him askant.
"What!" ejaculated Mr Pickwick. "And how long do you keep him out at a time?"
"Two or three weeks," replied the man.
"Weeks!" said Mr Pickwick in astonishment.
"He lives in Pentonwil when he's at home, but we seldom takes him home on account of his veakness. He always falls down when he's took out o' the cab, but when he's in it, we bears him up werry tight, and takes him in werry short, so he can't werry well fall down; and we've got a pair o' precious large wheels on, so ven he *does* move, they run after him, and he must go on – he can't help it . . ." '

They ignore the rain.

End of Scene One.

Later that afternoon.

The dining room of the boarding house. Large table and chairs.

Harley stands and waits. Dorothy enters with a tablecloth, which she spreads over the table.

Harley Would you like some help?

Dorothy You're a guest . . .

Short pause.

We're eating early tonight because of the play.

Harley Mr Spraight told me.

As Dorothy fixes the tablecloth:

Dorothy Have you seen the play *Twelfth Night* before?

Harley I have.

Dorothy Do you like it?

Harley I do. Very much.

Dorothy They don't have any women in it.

Harley I know. This is a men's college.

Dorothy Some men's colleges ask women from the town. Faculty wives . . . others. They don't do that here.

Frank enters from the hallway

Frank Henry's gone upstairs to change his clothes. He's been painting the scenery.

Dorothy is interested in this.

(*To Dorothy.*) Do you mind if we talk in here? It's still raining outside.

Dorothy No. I don't mind. I have to . . . (*set the table*)

Frank We understand. Here, let me –

Harley She doesn't want any help from the guests.

Short pause. They wait. Dorothy goes out to the kitchen. she will come in and out throughout the scene, setting the table, etc.

What did you tell him?

Frank That you just wanted to talk, that's all.

Harley You mentioned this teaching job –

Frank I did.

Harley The more I think about it, the less I . . .

Frank The less you what?

Harley I don't need a job. I have work I'm doing.

Frank (*quietly*) Just talk to him, Harley. What harm could it do?
   He said he wasn't even sure there was a job. there's just been a rumour. And he's not the one who hires anyway.

Harley Then why am I –?

Frank Just talk to him. He's a nice man. Where's the harm in that?

Short pause. They wait.
   They watch Dorothy set the table.

Harley I didn't even ask you how *Pickwick* went.

Frank Here he comes . . .

Henry Smith, thirty-nine, enters, smiling.

Henry Mr Barker, it was such a pleasant surprise to get your invitation.

Harley (*confused, to Frank*) My invitation?

Henry To have a chat.

Frank I told Professor Smith you wanted to have a talk.

Harley I do. I do. (*Beat.*) I've been here a month and we've hardly talked. I don't know why.

Dorothy Henry, could you help me set the table?

Frank Mrs Blackwell – we're talking with Henry.

Dorothy You want to talk to my brother?

Frank Yes. Yes, we do.

She goes off again into the kitchen.

Harley (*to the disappearing Dorothy*) Mrs Blackwell, could we get coffee?!

Henry I'll get it.

Frank (*stopping Henry*) No, no. Sit. I'll ask your sister. You two talk.

Frank goes off to the kitchen.
Short pause.

Henry It's an honour, Mr Barker. We're all nervous about you coming tonight.

Harley You shouldn't be.

Henry I'm sorry we haven't had the chance to talk before. Teaching – I think it eats up time. (*Smiles.*)

Harley I can imagine.

Frank returns.

Frank Coffee's coming. (*To Henry.*) I told Harley that you were probably not the one who does the hiring.

Henry Oh no. I'm not.

Awkward pause.

(*Noticing his dirty fingernails.*) I've been painting the scenery.

Frank And you are the director of tonight's performance?

Henry I am. Yes. Finally. They finally let me.

Harley It's a beautiful college. I've been here a while now and . . .

Henry I know that.

Harley Of course you do.

Henry (*to Frank*) We see each other every day.

Frank And now you get a chance to finally talk.

Another short, awkward pause.

Did you happen to see Harley's *Midsummer* in New York?

Henry I don't get to New York very often. (*Beat.*) I don't have the time.

Frank Harley – after I saw it – he told me what he wanted to do with the play.

Henry What do you mean?

Frank Why he did what he did. He . . . In the final scene? You know the play?

Henry (*of course*) It's Shakespeare.

Frank The court scene. He put everyone in a white box.

Harley Frank . . .

Henry Why did you do that?

Frank A big white box . . .

Harley So the actors could stand out.

I also did away with the footlights, and shone light directly from the lip of the balcony. I brought the actors to the very edge of the stage, as close as I could get them to the audience. And – with their backs to the audience. Those who were watching the clowns.

Henry is confused.

One of the young ushers came up to me . . . (*He smiles.*) I didn't tell you this, Frank. He said – 'Sir, did you know, that if that man' – one of the court – 'was turned around a little, we could see his face?' He seemed so proud with that observation. I said, 'But I don't want you to see *his* face.' (*Smiles.*)

Dorothy is back and is listening as she sets down the coffee, etc.

(*To Henry.*) Some people felt very uncomfortable.

Smiles, looks to Frank, then back to Henry.

I heard someone say – (*another smile*) 'How am I supposed to lose myself when right there is the sweaty neck of an actor?'

Looks to Frank, who smiles.

Henry Huh.

Dorothy Why did you do that?

They turn to her.

Henry In our *Twelfth Night* we use footlights. Is that wrong?

Harley No, no –

Henry (*over this*) Are you going to hate that?

28

Harley No, no . . . (*After a look at Frank.*) I'm not saying – I still use footlights too. I have. Not as much as I once . . . Mr Shaw, for instance, insists on them.

Dorothy (*holding up a cup*) Coffee?

She hands out and pours.

Henry I don't like Shaw's plays.

Harley I'm sure I'm going to enjoy *Twelfth Night* tonight very much. But what I'm saying is –

Frank What he's arguing for, Henry –

Henry He's arguing?

Harley No tricks. Nothing – 'clever'. I'm not being clear. For example, the Oberon. When he says – he is invisible. I didn't have him hide or run off or even turn his back. The other characters just didn't see him any more. Simple. Do you see what I mean?

Frank I liked that.

Harley And I think *that* should be taught to students. Be simple. And all that that says about stage design today.

He looks to Frank, who nods in agreement.

How since really the late seventeenth century, the theatre has struck up a rather doubtful alliance with scenic art and artists with a capital A.

He smiles. Frank smiles knowingly.

And all the harm that that has caused. We don't need revolving stages, and switchboards, and overly fancy lighting. It can be so much simpler than all of that. Someone should teach them that, that's all.

If someone isn't telling them in school, if all they learn about is what they see in the theatre today, most of which is rubbish, but we all know that, when plays are kept going now for months merely as 'the favour' of the shifting hotel populations, this is not what theatre can be. Must be. (*He has a new thought.*) Once, Henry, at a public dinner, an old playwright – I won't say which one – he's congratulated for the wonderful parts he's given actors. He stands up and shouts: 'Parts! I do not create parts! I create men and women!'

He smiles. Frank smiles.

That's what I mean. That's what I'd teach, what they need to know. If they are really interested in the theatre. Do you think your students would be interested in learning that?

Short pause.

Henry Most of our students go into business. (*Beat.*) Do you know what we pay, Mr Barker?

Harley I don't.

Harley looks to Frank.

Frank Harley told me that he has a passion for getting young people excited – 'a passion and a few boards!' (*Looks to Harley.*) Correct? (*To Henry.*) That's all one needs. The rest just gets in the way.

Short pause.

Henry Mrs French paints most of our scenery. I just helped out today because she was behind.

Harley I see.

Henry You should meet her. She's a very proficient painter. I think you'll see that tonight.

Harley I look forward to it.

Henry You know the drinking scene in *Twelfth Night*?

Harley Yes.

Henry My sister disagrees.

Dorothy (*setting the table*) I do.

Henry (*smiles to the others*) The wall? At the back? It looks completely real. Very – Tudor. She copied it off of a photograph. I don't know how she does it. You'll enjoy talking with her.

Harley So she will be there tonight?

Dorothy (*under her breath*) Oh yes . . .

Harley Good.

Henry She added a bookcase. To the wall. She loves doing bookcases – because of the different colours of the books, she says. (*Then to Frank.*) What does Mr Barker want to teach?

Frank Ask him.

Harley (*after a look at Frank*) I'm not . . .

Frank Harley isn't looking for a job, Henry. He's just curious.

Dorothy sits and joins them at the table, though at a bit of distance.

Henry Shakespeare? Are you saying you would teach Shakespeare?

Harley I could –

Frank Who better than Harley Granville Barker to –?

Henry Professor Weston already teaches Shakespeare. I once wanted to teach Shakespeare. (*To Dorothy.*) Didn't I? That was impossible, wasn't it? (*To Harley.*) You'll meet him tonight. He always stages the Shakespeare plays. But he's been ill, so that's why I . . . Professor Weston's been here for ever.

Dorothy Henry finally got his chance, Mr Barker. Though Mrs French still painted the scenery. No one else is allowed to. They don't even listen to you if you ask.

Frank So he should talk to Professor Weston.

Harley I will. Tonight.

Henry He's not going to want to talk to you though. I can see that already. He's going to say – (*To Dorothy.*) Isn't he?

She nods.

Harley What?

Henry 'What do we need you for? Shakespeare is already being taught here.' That's what we're all up against. (*To Dorothy.*) Isn't it?

Dorothy It is.

Henry Let me think. (*To Dorothy.*) He's going to do everything in his power to stop him from teaching Shakespeare.

She nods.

(*To Harley.*) You have to realise that. At first he *seems* like a nice man.

Harley I don't have to teach Shake—

Henry Dorothy, what about this?

Dorothy What?

Henry turns to Harley.

Henry The most popular career for a graduate of this school twenty years ago – do you know what it was? The ministry. The school has worked very hard to change that. Not that we have anything against the ministry, but – the school figured this out – ministers usually aren't terribly well off. (*Laughs to himself.*) And therefore . . .

Harley What?

Henry Not in a position . . .

Harley (*confused*) To what?

Dorothy (*she gets what he is saying*) To 'give back' to their old college.

Henry But now that it's 'business' – as the popular career – we suddenly have an endowment.

Harley (*very confused*) I don't understand what this has to do with what we're talking about?

Henry The theatre, Mr Barker. Your profession. It's – exciting. Especially to young men. Wealthy young men. They like to hang around the theatre. Do you see where I'm headed?

Harley No.

Henry You are very well regarded, are you not?

Frank He is.

Henry Well known. In the theatre world. So – if we were fortunate enough to engage you to teach here, we could make the argument that just your presence here might attract a few more wealthy young men as students. Who would then in turn, after they graduate, either they or their fathers – would 'help out' their old school.

Smiles, pleased with the idea, looks to Dorothy, who nods.

(*To Dorothy.*) Professor Weston would have a hell of a hard time answering that one. (*Laughs to himself. Then:*) You need to insist on teaching Shakespeare. Don't settle for anything less. (*To Dorothy.*) Professor Weston will be fit to be tied. (*Big smile.*)

Harley I'm not looking for a job –

Henry Just don't expect applause. Teaching's not like that. It's hard work.

Frank He doesn't expect – applause. Do you?

Frank looks at Harley.

Harley told me – just before I went to find you, Henry – he said what he really wanted now was to find out where the Goths went when they vanished out of Italy . . .

Harley Frank –

Henry What?

Frank He means he wants to read long books about – Byzantium. To – think again for thinking's sake alone.

Henry That's – (*Looks for the word.*) Noble. (*Shrugs, then:*) When I first arrived here, at this college, I happened to mention at a meeting that I'd love to one day teach Shakespeare. Weston then just made my life unbearable. You can't imagine how petty some people can be.

Harley People can be petty in the theatre.

Frank Why do we keep talking about this professor?

Henry (*continuing*) He criticised me to my students. He'd find out what classroom I wanted, and he'd take it from me. I had trouble getting books I needed. I'm sure it was him. Finally I just bit the bullet and went to him and apologised.

It wasn't enough. His pride had been hurt, I guess. (*Shrugs.*) He hadn't punished me enough yet? That's when he asked my sister – (*looks to Dorothy*) to help

Mrs French paint the scenery for Cap and Bells. I thought that was a nice thing. Until he'd humiliate her too – tell her to repaint things. Make fun of her. 'This woman,' he'd say, in front of the boys –

It was all to get back at me. it would have gone on and on, but I went to one of his Shakespeare classes. And afterward, I walked up to him and said quite loudly so others could hear – 'I don't know what I could have been thinking, I could never teach Shakespeare like you.' That – ended it.

He sips his coffee.

He'll put up a fight, Mr Barker. He's already asked me two or three times – what is Granville Barker doing in Williamstown? And what is he doing living in your sister's boarding house?

You've made him nervous. and that man, when nervous – is dangerous. (*To Frank.*) You're lucky. He doesn't like Dickens.

Harley (*smiling*) I'm not after anything.

Short pause. Henry looks to Dorothy, then to Harley.

Henry He talks about you. About you and your work.

Harley About me? What about me?

Henry (*hesitates, then*) You did some plays in college baseball stadiums?

Harley Outdoors. Yes. Greek plays. As they were done when they were written.

Henry He has friends, Mr Barker. One of his friends from Yale? You were there?

Harley I did two Greek plays in the Yale Bowl.

Henry Right. (*To Dorothy.*) So he got that right. (*Then to Harley.*) And – he'd heard that when the sun set behind the stadium? The men in the crowd stood up to put on their jackets, because it was colder now? And people started shouting: 'Seventh Inning Stretch!' Like at a baseball game. In the middle of *Medea*? People laughed, guffawed, made noises –

Harley And some people were moved.

Henry shrugs. Pause.

Henry Whatever happened – this is what Weston is telling people. You are the butt of his joke.

They sip their coffees.

Dorothy My brother is a playwright too.

Henry I used to be.

Frank I didn't know that.

Henry Mr Barker and I actually shared a producer. Mr Frohman?

Dorothy Mr Frohman produced my brother's play.

Henry *Suki.* Have you heard of it?

Harley I'm sorry, I don't think I have.

Dorothy It's a comedy.

Henry (*correcting her*) A farce, Dorothy.

Dorothy A farce. Suki's – she's a model. She has only the one name.

Henry I don't think they're interested.

Dorothy Of course they are. They're in the theatre business, Henry. (*Continuing about Suki.*) She speaks in – jargon. Suki. (*Smiles at a remembered line.*) And wrecks an automobile and needs money to fix it. So she pretends to be a famous foreign painter. Goes to New Jersey – (*To Henry.*) What's the place called again?

Henry (*smiling*) 'Parnassus Towers'.

Dorothy 'Parnassus Towers, New Jersey.' (*She laughs.*)
He made that up. To this rich woman who helps artists.
And very funny things happen . . . (*Then to Henry.*) And
there's a love story too.

Henry It played the Lyceum. For a couple of weeks. Mr
Frohman produced it.

Dorothy Then he left on the *Lusitania*.

Henry I used to stand in the back of the theatre. My
mouth – open. (*To Harley.*) You know what that's like.
Ann Murdock played Suki?

Pause. Turns to Dorothy.

What about a drink, Dorothy? (*To the men.*) And then
I was offered this job at the college.

*Dorothy gets up and goes off to get a bottle and
glasses.*

(*Continuing.*) And one of the first things I did was show
Weston my play. He'd mentioned how much he likes to
read new plays. How he 'knows' Professor Baker – who
teaches plays at Harvard? How he 'had a good eye' for
this sort of thing.

Frank Weston?

Henry Yes. He kept saying – if he didn't have the scruples,
he'd be a producer. And be rich. (*Beat.*) He said some
nice things about *Suki*. So I gave him a second play that
hadn't been done yet. I thought it might be nice for the
students to read a brand new play. Or even, if they liked
it, perform it as one of the Cap and Bells productions. I
mean – I am teaching here. I thought it would be a treat.

*Dorothy has returned and is pouring drinks for the
men.*

Weston urged them to do it. 'Let's put it on!' he said. And he staged it himself. (*Drinks.*) He staged it very, very badly. On purpose, I now think. He didn't want a successful playwright in the department. No one liked it. Even if one or two people told me they did. I knew.

Short pause.

Dorothy My brother staged the play tonight. It's the first time Professor Weston has allowed him to do that. I think it's a trap.

Henry shrugs.
Charles appears in the doorway.

Henry (*before he can go out again*) Charles, what are you doing here?

Charles I was just . . .

Henry (*standing up and looking out of a window*) Isn't it still raining?

Dorothy Is it?

Henry He isn't wet? Why isn't your jacket wet?

They look at him.

Charles (*a bad liar*) I don't know.

Frank (*helping out*) Perhaps it stopped and just started again.

Awkward moment. then Beatrice appears behind Charles.

Beatrice What's happening?

Henry (*confused*) What's going on? I don't understand.

Dorothy (*lying*) Charles has come to pick you up for rehearsal, Henry.

The others, except Henry, realise that Dorothy knows about Charles and Beatrice.

Mrs Hale, Henry, must have just come in as well. And she isn't wet either. See. It must have stopped.

Beatrice It has. It did.

They all hear the rain outside.

It's started up again. Thank you, Mrs Blackwell, for – explaining.

Henry What time is it? (*Checks his watch.*) Charles, we don't do our Italian rehearsal for another hour and a half . . .

Dorothy (*to Henry*) He must have got confused, Henry.

Charles I got confused. I should come back.

Beatrice (*stopping him*) Wait. Perhaps Charles could have dinner with us? Would that be possible?

Dorothy I don't think that's –

Frank (*to Beatrice*) Don't –

Charles (*over this*) I shouldn't –

Beatrice He's here.

Frank Beatrice –

Beatrice (*maybe too forcefully*) Why do you have to go? (*Realises maybe she is being too forceful.*) But maybe you have plans for dinner.

Henry (*smiling*) Perhaps there's a girl.

Beatrice I don't think there's a girl. (*Then, to Charles.*) Do you?

Charles No.

39

Beatrice So he doesn't have plans. Mrs Blackwell? Frank, he doesn't have plans.

Henry (*smiling*) Of course, come in.

Takes Charles by the arm.

We have room. We have enough, don't we, Dorothy? (*Looks to Dorothy.*)

Dorothy I'll get a plate for Charles.

It is now pouring outside. Dorothy stops and listens.

You're so lucky to have just missed the rain, Mrs Hale.

She goes off.

Henry And Charles, you too. Good thing he came early.

Short pause.

Harley (*to say something*) So – what is an Italian rehearsal? I don't think I know.

Charles When you do all the lines as fast as you can.

Henry And the staging. You don't do Italian rehearsals in England?

Harley (*thinks, then*) Not often enough.

Henry It helps the boys limber their mouths.

Dorothy returns with another place-setting.

Beatrice (*out of nowhere*) I hope it's all right that I asked Charles. He looks . . . hungry. (*She smiles.*)

Dorothy (*not looking at him*) Are you hungry, Charles?

Charles I am. I'm starved.

Dorothy (*to herself, mumbles*) What a surprise . . . Henry . . . Please, help.

Dorothy goes back to the kitchen. Henry reorganises the table for one more.
   Awkward moment, then:

Beatrice (*to Charles, she can't help it*) You've missed a button.

All but Henry are aware of him now buttoning the missed button on his shirt.

(*To change the subject*) So, Henry – how long has your sister been a widow?

Henry Seven years.

Beatrice And she's still in mourning. And she's so young.

Dorothy comes out with silverware, a bowl, etc.

Henry (*to Dorothy*) Should I call George?

Dorothy He'll be down as soon as he smells food. (*To the others.*) He never misses a free meal . . .

She goes off again.

Beatrice Did he teach here? Her husband?

Henry Biology . . .

Harley So why does she still wear black? (*A joke.*) She's 'in mourning for her life'? (*He laughs.*)

Henry What?

No one understands.

Harley A play I saw . . . I'm sorry.

Beatrice (*continuing*) It is a long time.

Henry There's a reason. She isn't coming back . . . (*He looks over his shoulder to make sure.*) After Professor Blackwell, her husband, suddenly died . . . And this was long before I started teaching here . . .

Dorothy returns with more bowls, etc., and Henry suddenly changes the subject:

You are all seeing the play tonight?

Harley I am. Of course.

Frank It's his second *Twelfth Night* this week. (*Explaining to Henry.*) Holyoke.

Dorothy Did you see that, Charles?

Charles No.

Dorothy goes out again.

Henry (*continuing*) He died and at the funeral everyone's there. And so forth and so on. Then my sister hears that there's going to be another service for him – a sort of memorial – to which she has not been invited. It's on the other side of the campus. Five-minute walk. In another woman's house.

Dorothy returns again. Now suspicious.

Dorothy What are you talking about?

No one knows what to say.

Frank The weather . . . Is it raining?

Dorothy (*about the sound of the rain*) What is that? It's pouring outside.

The others look off to the window.

Frank (*to Charles*) Good thing it's not a Greek play.

Charles What? Why?

Frank Harley did all those Greek plays outside. Did it ever rain on one of those, Harley?

Dorothy heads back into the kitchen.

Henry (*continuing*) Another woman. And my sister's husband, it turns out, lived with this woman too over many years. Five minutes away. I suppose it was convenient. And everyone knew. Of course. You couldn't hide that. Not on a college campus.

Beatrice No. That would be hard.

Harley looks at Beatrice.

Henry Everyone knew except my sister. And no one told her. Professor Weston said it was because no one liked her. She didn't fit in. She was 'uppity', he said. She thought maybe it was the accent.

So she tried to lose her accent. She worked at that. But then she didn't.

Beatrice Or maybe decided she didn't want to.

Henry We came over as children years and years ago.

Frank We're all English.

Beatrice Not Charles.

Henry Anyway, my sister learns of this memorial service and discovers everything. (*Shrugs, then:*) She dressed all in black. And so did this other lady. And so that's how they both still dress. I see her – the other one – all the time in town. It's become a kind of competition, I guess. Who's going to end their mourning first. Who's going to give up.

Short pause.

Beatrice (*to Charles*) Did you know this?

He nods.

Charles Everyone does.

Henry I didn't know about any of it until I started teaching here. Professor Weston said she just should have moved away . . . I guess he didn't like seeing her.

43

Dorothy returns with more bowls of food.

Dorothy We can sit down now.

Pause. No one knows what to say. Dorothy puts out the food.

Henry, would you . . .?

Henry Of course.

He goes off into the kitchen, as the others choose their places.

Charles Where should I . . .?

Dorothy I'm assuming next to Mrs Hale.

Beatrice (*'smiling'*) That would be a treat. I'd like that.

Short pause.

Dorothy Mr Spraight – a telegram just came for you.

She takes it out of her apron pocket and hands it to him.

(*Explaining to the others.*) They know to come to the kitchen. That's where I always am . . .

Frank (*as he opens the telegram*) Where do you want me?

Then George enters, all smiles.

George That smells good!

Frank George. Dorothy was right.

George Right about what? This smells good. (*To Charles.*) What are you doing here?

Beatrice He's my guest.

Frank moves away from the table as he reads the telegram.

George So what has everyone been doing today? What did I miss?

Beatrice It was raining. It still is.

George So you stayed in?

Beatrice looks at Dorothy.

What? I think I'm missing something.

Dorothy Pass the plates . . .

Food is being dished out, etc. Harley looks to Frank reading the telegram.

Harley Frank, what it is?

Frank re-reads the telegram.

George Dorothy, I ran into Professor Weston in town. He said he had heard from two or three students how impressed they were with my talk. (*Smiles.*)

Harley (*as food is passed, still looking at Frank*) This is the one about the books Shakespeare had as a boy . . .?

George That's right. You've heard about it?

Beatrice How do you know what the boy Shakespeare read?

Harley That's what I was wondering.

George (*putting food on his plate*) I say 'could have'. 'Could have.'

Henry has returned with a big dish.

Dorothy (*to Henry*) George ran into Professor Weston. He heard nice things about his talk.

Henry Good for you.

Frank (*putting the telegram away and taking his place at the table*) I have a sick wife. (*To Beatrice.*) She's been sick . . . (*To Harley.*) Good days, bad days . . .

Beatrice How much time before the play?

George We have plenty of time.

Frank As it turns out I won't be seeing the play tonight.

George Why? Why not?

Frank I'm sorry, Henry.

The others are very surprised.

I need to head home.

Beatrice Tonight?

Frank (*shrugs, 'what can I do?'*) I have a sick wife.

Frank nods to Harley.

Harley I'm sorry, Frank.

Frank So I'll eat and run. Forgive me, everyone.

Short pause. They eat.

George (*eating*) What's wrong with your wife? If you don't mind my asking.

Short pause.

Dorothy Maybe he doesn't want to talk about it, George.

They eat in silence as the lights fade to black.

End of Scene Two.

The same, later in the meal. The room has got darker.
It's hard to see, though they don't seem to notice at first.
Charles is standing, in the middle of his demonstration
of an 'Italian rehearsal' of his character, Feste, in Twelfth
Night. *The others are laughing. He speaks the lines and*
does the 'business' as fast as he can.

Charles (*as fast as he can*) 'When that I was a little tiny
boy, with hey, ho, the wind and the rain, a foolish thing
was but a toy, for the rain it raineth every day –'

Henry (*seriously*) Don't breathe!

Charles (*without breathing*) 'But when I came to man's
estate with hey ho the wind and the rain 'gainst knaves
and thieves men shut their gate for the rain it raineth
every day!'

He takes a breath. Others applaud and cheer this feat.

I breathed once. Just once.

Then he takes a huge breath, and:

'But when I came alas to wive – ?'

Beatrice That's enough. He's going to hurt himself.
(*Smiles. To Charles.*) You looked like you were hurting
yourself.

Charles I wasn't.

The others applaud, etc.

Beatrice I think they're making fun of you.

Harley We're not. (*To Frank.*) Are we?

Frank No. I'm not.

Charles (*feeling his mouth*) My mouth feels like rubber.

Harley Is that good?

Charles Last week at rehearsal Professor Smith had Tom do 'If music be the food of love' – the whole thing, without breathing once. We thought he'd burst. (*Then, proudly.*) We're ready for tonight.

    Pause. They eat.

Harley I'm looking forward to it. A shame you'll miss it, Frank.

Frank My loss.

Henry I also have the whole cast sit in the empty theatre and just look at the stage. I want them to be aware of how they look.

    He eats.

Harley (*a toast*) Good luck.

    They toast.

Henry Thank you.

Harley I always preach that Shakespeare should be done at a good clip.

Beatrice How long is the performance?

Frank Sounds like about ten minutes.

    Laughter.

George When I was at university, I was in a play once. (*He smiles: this is a funny story.*) One of the third years wrote it. If you looked at the first letter of every line – just took those letters, they spelled out the name of certain professors. And then a comment. Say – Jones. And then – stupid. (*Smiles.*) The first letter – not counting character names. (*Eats.*)

48

Beatrice How did anyone just watching it – get that?

George They couldn't.

Short pause.

Beatrice Charles was telling me – earlier today – that many of the young men are going to some sort of summer camp.

Henry (*innocently, eating*) When was he telling you this?

Charles Plattsburgh.

Harley What for?

Beatrice A military camp.

Harley I see. (*To Charles.*) Are you going?

Beatrice His father would have a fit. I told him that.

Dorothy (*to Henry*) She knows his father.

Beatrice Did I tell you that?

Charles Professor Shephard's been teaching a class on military tactics.

George (*to Henry*) Who's Shephard?

Dorothy (*before Henry can answer*) History.

Charles We meet at night twice a week. Once a week a real Army officer comes on campus and we go through 'tactical' walks. Around Williamstown.

Frank What does that mean?

Charles In case of attack. What would *we* do?

Frank Who's attacking Williamstown?

Beatrice That's what I said.

Charles (*over this*) It's interesting just to think about. So by the summer we – those in this group – we think we'll

49

be able to jump over the – 'beginners'. (*Big smile.*) Last week we started to drill. It's fun. It's like a play.

Beatrice No, it's not.

Short pause. Beatrice is upset.

Charles (*to Beatrice*) I know what I'm doing. My father might not think so, but I do.

Beatrice Mr Barker was just in France.

Harley It's not like Williamstown . . .

Dorothy (*standing*) It's gotten dark. (*To Henry.*) Shouldn't we light the candles?

Frank (*pointing to the overhead lamps*) Can't we just turn on the lamps?

Henry They don't work –

Charles (*to the table, continuing*) We had a speaker . . .

Beatrice Oh good.

Henry (*to Frank, about the lights*) We can't afford to get them fixed. They put them in wrong. (*To Dorothy.*) Didn't they?

Dorothy We don't know that. (*Handing Henry matches.*) Henry . . .

Henry I think they cheated us.

George (*taking the matches*) I'll do it . . .

Beatrice (*to Charles*) What about this 'speaker'?

Charles He told us what to expect from the camp. He had slides.

Beatrice 'smiles' at this.

Why is that funny?

Beatrice (*to the table*) Oh he had 'slides'.

George begins to light the candles on the table, and their faces suddenly start to become brighter.

Charles If you are not going to listen . . .
We'll get up at 5:45 in the morning. Start with callisthenics. And we can choose – engineering, signalling, artillery, cavalry. We do our own cooking.

Beatrice Like boy scouts. Why don't you join them?

Charles Because I'm not a boy!

Short pause.

Beatrice No. No, you're not.

Charles (*continues to the table*) How to scout. Work under fire. Attack and retreat.
One of the seniors – he left in the fall and joined with – (*gestures around the table*) the English. He wrote to the newspaper. He's already been involved in three great battles in – (*gestures to Harley*) France. He said – you learn to tell what sort of shells they're firing by the marks they leave on tree trunks. That was interesting.

Frank (*to Henry*) Harley was recently in France writing a book.

Harley (*shrugs*) Not fighting. (*Smiles.*) In London it's . . . chaotic. A bomb landed just down the road from – where my wife lives.

George That must have been frightening. Was she scared? Did she say?

Harley She didn't. Friends of hers wrote to me about it.

Charles You know who his wife is, don't you?

Beatrice We do, Charles. We do.

George You should bring her to New York. You shouldn't be the only one who's safe.

Harley I'm not here to be safe. Like Charles, I'm not frightened by this war. As senseless as it seems to be. I'm not here because of that.

Short pause.
Henry takes out his watch.

Henry Maybe we should go, Charles. I said we'd start the rehearsal . . .

Looks at his watch.
Charles starts to pick up a plate.

Dorothy I'll pick up.

Charles grabs a piece of bread.

Beatrice Take more. You can't act on an empty stomach.

Harley That's not true for English actors . . .

Charles I'm full, really. Thank you for inviting me to dinner.

Dorothy Thank Mrs Hale.

Beatrice Good luck, young Feste. And you too, Henry.

Henry I am a little bit nervous.

Charles I'm not.

Henry (*to Beatrice*) You must feel that all the time.

Beatrice Yes, I'm nervous – all the time.

Frank He meant when you act.

Harley It hits me in the stomach. I have a very bad stomach . . .

They all laugh, and Charles and Henry go off.

Beatrice (*cries out*) Goodbye! (*Beat.*) Thank God this country isn't at war yet . . .

Frank Sooner or later.

Harley Later. Later's always better . . .

Beatrice Excuse me . . .

She gets up and hurries out after them.

George What is she doing?

No response.

Dorothy Who wants something else?
Besides Mrs Hale.

George finishes eating.

George I think I'll go with them . . . (*To Dorothy.*) Do you mind?

Dorothy Go.

George Professor Weston said he was going to be there early.

Dorothy I understand.

George It's always good to keep talking . . . So he remembers who I am? (*Smiles.*) Gentlemen, I'll see you later. I'll catch up with them. I don't want to arrive just by myself. That always looks bad. Like you're desperate.

He hurries out.

Harley See you there.

Frank (*calling after him*) I'll be gone . . .

But George is gone.

Harley (*to Frank*) Why do you think they call it an 'Italian' rehearsal?

Frank Because Italians speak so fast?

Harley Perhaps they don't breathe as often as we do . . . (*Smiles.*) I'm sorry about your wife. Does this happen often? Perhaps, Frank, she just misses you.

Beatrice has returned. They look at her.

Beatrice (*sitting back at the table*) I wanted to wish him well. Them. Both of them. I didn't think I had. Properly.

She takes a sip of wine.

Dorothy I think something bad's going to happen.

They all look at her.

I heard that Professor Weston is going to give a talk – after tonight's show.

Harley You think he'll criticise –?

Dorothy Not the students. He knows better.

Pause as they finish up eating.

Harley (*finally, to Dorothy*) When's the last train back to New York? For Frank?

Frank I'm going to take the night steamer. (*To Dorothy.*) I have all the timetables.

Beatrice Won't that take hours longer?
 I love that trip . . . . if you have the time.

Frank I'm home by morning.

Harley And that's all right?
 When do you have to – (*leave*)?

Frank I have time. I didn't really unpack.

Dorothy (*standing*) Anyone want anything else?

No response.
 She starts clearing the table.

Frank My wife and I took the night steamer up to Albany when we first arrived here. A friend told us we had to do that. Breathtaking. And huge. A river like that in Europe – it'd be famous. Our best day in America. (*Smiles.*)

Beatrice She'll get better. This is just a scare.

Frank I've told her I would take her back to England. Before it was too late. (*Beat.*) She appreciated that. I promised.

Beatrice Isn't that dangerous – for you? They're going to introduce general conscription any day, I'm told.

Harley Frank's too old –

Frank (*to Beatrice*) Do *you* want to die here?

Short pause.

Look at us. How did we all get here? (*To Dorothy who has come back from the kitchen.*) How did you get here, Mrs Blackwell? You've been here for ever we're told.

Dorothy I haven't. Not for ever. Not yet.

She takes more plates away.

Beatrice (*pointing to herself*) Six years.

Frank What?

Beatrice I have been here for six years. You asked – I was acting in *The Mollusc*. They wanted me to come over with it. I felt I needed to get out of my uncle's shadow.

Harley So you're still acting. I didn't know.

Beatrice No. No, I'm not.
Just in life . . . (*Smiles.*) I do some lecturing. Like you. Mostly girls' schools . . . I can't seem to break into the men's colleges.

Harley At least not as a lecturer . . .

She smiles.

Beatrice Mr Barker?

Harley One month! I'm still a tourist!

Frank Eleven years. I don't even remember why.

Harley (*to Frank*) Apparently when the conscription bill is passed, technically – we're not subject to it. Because we're not there. So – should we go back, we'd be treated as volunteers who can choose how we wish to serve. And perhaps thus avoid the trenches.

Frank I didn't know that. Thank you.

Harley Every letter I get mentions someone who's died.

Short pause.

Frank To change the subject . . . I read an article in the student newspaper –

Harley You were reading that all morning. How interesting could it be?

Frank It's interesting. A glimpse into another world. Like reading Dickens. And this article was interesting. About someone from another college who came and gave a talk about how art, or being an artist, is not really a good choice of career for a young man. How there's little money in it. How it all lacks a, quote, 'sound economic basis'. And how there isn't even any honour in it either . . . He ended up, the speaker, by saying if you have to do art, then – get a real job first.
Spoken, it sounded like, with an element of pity.

Harley It's not an easy life. (*To Beatrice.*) Does Charles really want to be an actor?

Beatrice He does. He thinks he does. (*Smiles. Shrugs.*)

Harley Good for him. We need good actors.

I think it's actors that I most admire. They seem the least – cynical of us in the theatre 'business'. They are what I most remember . . . When I think about something I've seen. When it's right – there's a real intimacy. You're in the same room with them. A very human art. When it's right. I'm boring you.

Beatrice No.

Frank No.

Harley I've thought of trying to write a play – against everything that's in Aristotle. Where there wouldn't be any 'doing'. Only 'being'. And so the job of the actor would be to interest the audience not in what his character did, but who he was. As in life. That would be a real achievement, I think.

Beatrice (*eating*) Interesting.

Frank (*eating*) That is.

   Pause.

Sometimes I feel so far away here.

Harley From what, Frank – home? And what's that?

Frank I sit in rooming houses, look out windows. It's raining. It's not raining. It's snowing. I go out and speak – *Pickwick*. I also do *A Tale of Two Cities*. It's lonely I suppose is what I'm saying. (*Looks at the others.*) I came here for a reason. I know that. Both of us did. But I don't remember any more what that was. Was I looking for something?

I'm sorry. I don't know why I'm talking like this.

   Dorothy had returned and had stopped what she was doing to listen to this. She now continues to clean off the table.

Beatrice I remember the good things of England. Not what it was really like. Just good things. I have to tell myself that.

Frank I feel a hole. (*Points to his chest.*) And as if I could taste something, but not allowed to eat it. Or it's kept out of my reach? Or perhaps it's lost?

Harley You're worried about your wife.

Frank hesitates.

Frank (*quietly*) I'm not worried about my wife.

He looks at Harley.

Harley I often feel like I'm missing something. But I feel that at home too.

Frank I sometimes think this country is like one of those great Shakespearean forests – where you enter it and you change. And at the same time you know nothing about it is real.

Pause.

Harley Speaking of Shakespeare, I am looking forward to the play tonight.

Beatrice (*smiling*) So am I.

Dorothy Charles plays the clown?

Beatrice He's going to be good. I've heard him do a couple of speeches.

Dorothy You were helping him practise?

Beatrice I was.

Frank (*over this*) I'm sorry I won't . . .

Harley I'll write and tell you about it. (*To Beatrice.*) I told Frank, I saw a *Twelfth Night* a week or so ago at Holyoke.

Beatrice You said. I've lectured there. It's all girls.

Harley And it was only girls in the play. It was – (*seeks the right word, then:*) terrible. (*Laughs.*) And wonderful. I don't know what they understood, or had been told – how many Italian rehearsals they'd been subjected to – but I was moved. Not by the art. But perhaps this is just sentimental – and I think it is, and so something to fight, but – when I can't give myself one reason why I should continue making theatre . . . . (*Short pause.*) I can't even now remember why I started in the first place. What I found once, which I've obviously lost . . .

My friend Archer told me that the theatres in London are full right now – with patriotic songs and patriotic plays and . . . and things that say only what an audience already thinks.

I was saying, those girls in *Twelfth Night*, as Malvolio, Sir Toby, as the women . . . it *was* moving. And I'm never moved in theatre any more. Why? Why?

Then on the train back here, from Holyoke and that wonderful girl Malvolio. (*Smiling, laughs to himself.*) I suddenly remember something. When I was a boy, and my mother sent me to acting school . . . I didn't go to any other school. Acting school in Margate.

Frank Margate?

Harley I know – the ugliest beach in England.

Frank I don't think so. (*To Beatrice.*) My wife came from near there. I haven't heard that name for ages . . . Margate . . .

Harley 'Oh to Margate! To Margate!' (*Smiles.*)

Frank What?

Harley Nothing. (*Continues.*) I'd been helping my mother on stage for my whole life.

Beatrice What did your mother do?

Harley Sang a little. Mostly – she did bird calls.

Beatrice Bird calls?

Harley shrugs.

Harley It was a different time. So it all was a business for me from the very beginning. And now I was being sent to school to learn more about the business. I was impatient – even competitive, highly critical – especially if the other students didn't take the business as seriously as I did.

One day around Christmas, and we were all living in the same house. All the boys. We are called from our rooms down into the parlour. and as we all sat down, through the doorway – (*points*) came St George on his horse.

Beatrice The Mummers.

Harley Of course the horse was attached to him.

Frank I remember the Mummers.

Beatrice I loved the Mummers . . .

Harley And then a dragon. Two men. And they fought; the dragon died. A doctor came in.

Beatrice I remember. I do . . .

Harley And he healed the dragon and then they all danced and sang. I loved it.

Beatrice I remember being ill one Christmas. And when the Doctor healed the knights and the dragon – I became better too. Why was that? (*She smiles.*)

Harley When they were gone, I asked our head of the house, this woman, retired actress I think – what theatre they were with. Oh, she says, they're not with any theatre, son. That one there – he was the butcher. And St George – the schoolteacher. And the Mayor, and so on . . .

'How much did you have to pay them?' I asked her. She looked at me, rubbed my head, and said – 'We pay them nothing. We don't pay. We give a drink. A cake.' I was incredulous. Then – I ask, 'Why do they do it?'

'They just do,' she says.

Pause.

Beatrice My mother used to give our Mummers little biscuits wrapped in a ribbon. I always tied the ribbons . . .

Short pause.

Are there Mummers – (*here*)?

Dorothy No.

They all turn and see she has been standing and listening, plates in hand.

Beatrice Why not, I wonder.

Dorothy It's an English thing.

She now goes off into the kitchen.
Short pause.

Beatrice (*looks at her watch*) We still have a few minutes.

Short pause.

(*To Frank.*) Which lecture bureau, Frank? I meant to ask before.

Frank Who sends me out?

Beatrice Yes.

Frank (*gestures to him and Harley*) We're both with J. B. Pond.

Beatrice Is Pond the one in the Metropolitan Life Building?

Harley (*nods*) Pond's son runs it now. James Jr. But it's still fine.

Beatrice I think I've met him. I think he approached me. But you like him?

Harley He's all right. And you?

Beatrice Mr Feakins. In the Times Building.

Harley I know.

Beatrice Redpath has also approached me.

Pause. No one knows what to do, then Frank stands up.

Frank I should get my bag. I need to go.

He stops. Dorothy returns.

Here we are – three English people. We found each other. On the edge of the earth . . .

He goes off to get his bag.

Beatrice Poor man. He's so worried about his wife . . .

Harley He is.

Dorothy She's dead.

Harley What, Mrs Blackwell?

Dorothy I read the telegram. The boy had the name confused so I thought I should check.
She's died. His wife.

Beatrice And he knows this?

Dorothy It's in the telegram.

Short pause.

Harley (*to himself*) Good God . . .

Beatrice How awful . . . (*To say something, to Harley.*)
So you're happy with him? Pond? The son?

Harley Who's happy with their agent?

Beatrice Feakins gets me jobs – I'll get a lecture say in
Albany. At Emma Willard School. On a Tuesday. Then
he'll book me in – I don't know – Saratoga on the
Friday.

Frank returns now with this bag.
   *Beatrice stops, doesn't know what to say, then
continues to Harley.*

I try and tell Feakins, what am I supposed to do between
Tuesday and Friday? Sit all alone in a hotel room?

Harley We're still complaining about our lecture
bureaus, Frank. Is Redpath the biggest? I'm not sure.

Frank I think it is.

Beatrice Is that good? To be the biggest?

Frank It can be. It cannot be. Pond is smallish. I think
we both mostly deal with Pond Jr. himself, Harley, don't
we?

Harley And he sort of specialises in English lecturers.

Frank He has a few.

Beatrice Laurence Housman's with Feakins.

Harley I knew that.

Dorothy I read the telegram, Mr Spraight. I'm sorry. I
told them . . .

Pause.

63

Frank Harley – perhaps I'll see you in New York. Or back here if you're still around. I come through all the time. Beatrice . . .

They don't shake hands.
Frank goes.

Dorothy (*as she takes the last of the dishes off to the kitchen*) Should we blow these out? (*The candles.*) Aren't you going soon?

She goes out.

Harley (*calling after her*) We're going right now, Mrs Blackwell. (*Starts to stand.*) We need to get good seats.

Beatrice Charles organised seats. You're an important guest.

Harley What about you?

Beatrice I think we're sitting together.

They are about to leave when Dorothy returns for the last of the dishes.

Dorothy (*entering*) Let me know how her scenery looks. She's done the same Tudor room with the bookcases in at least four other plays.

They go.
Dorothy blows out the candles. The room is dark. She takes the last dishes back into the kitchen.

End of Scene Three.

SCENE FOUR

The same, that night, after the play. Light from the hallway; the room is dark.

Dorothy sits alone in the shadows, smoking. Somewhere off in the distance, across campus, there is music playing – a band for dancing. The rain stopped a while ago.

Sound of the front door opening and then slamming shut, and first a shadow of a figure in the light from the hallway. Then Harley enters. He tosses down his hat. He doesn't see Dorothy.

Harley goes to a chair, sighs and sits listening to the music for a moment when he suddenly feels Dorothy's presence and, startled, turns:

Harley Who's there?

He reaches into his pocket for matches, and as he lights a lamp on a table:

Mrs Blackwell. I didn't see you. You scared me. (*He 'smiles'.*) You're sitting in the dark.

No response.

God, it was stuffy in that theatre.

Dorothy Was it?

Harley Sticky. Nice to get some air. I was listening to the music.

Dorothy (*quietly*) What happened?

He hesitates.

Harley What do you mean?

She just looks at him.

The air always feels – fresher. After rain, doesn't it . . .
A little humid still . . .

Dorothy Mr Barker, what happened?

Harley You mean the play?

No response.

It was perfectly all right. They had a good time. (*Smiles.*)
Henry should be pleased.
    I told him that. I'm not sure he listened . . . The
scenery was nicely painted. (*Smiles.*) I'm sure it could
have been better . . . More original. (*Looks off, then:*)
I don't think Charles Massinger was very good. I don't
think he should be an actor . . . But he'll discover that
for himself. One way or the other.

She just looks at him, waiting.

Would you like more light?

Dorothy Where's my brother?

Harley I don't know. I suspect he'll be home soon.
Professor Weston is having a party – (*Hearing the
music.*) That could be it . . . Or is that one of those
fraternity parties . . . ? (*Shrugs.*)

Dorothy I see.

Harley But I don't think Henry was planning to go.

Dorothy No.

Short pause. The music in the distance.
    Dorothy stands.

I should leave you alone.

Harley You were right. Professor Weston took charge.
He tried to be very nice to me. Introduced me to the
students as a friend. (*Shrugs, shakes his head: 'amazing'.*)

66

Said – (*incredulous*) perhaps we would work together on something. Someday. In the theatre. Perhaps in London, he said . . .

Why would I do that?

She sits back down.

He made a welcoming speech. Never once mentioned Henry. The play went off well. (*Shrugs.*) They were students having fun. Then after . . . Some of the audience left. I think mostly the public. But the students and other teachers and . . . (*Shrugs.*) They stayed to hear what Weston had to say. It was as if they all knew – And no one wanted to miss out. And Weston spoke. And he was – cruel.

Dorothy flinches.

I'm sorry . . .

Short pause.

You were correct. Weston never criticised a student. But he made fun of Henry. Of his – ideas for the play. Asked Henry, in front of us, if he actually had read it all the way through. *Twelfth Night.* He has a way of saying something, and then poking his tongue into his cheek. Weston?

Dorothy nods, she has seen this.

It gives the impression that he's condescending to everything, and making sure we understand that. If I ever do a production of *Richard III*, I will insist that the actor speak and then poke his tongue into his cheek. (*Smiles.*) What else? He took some of the students, the actors, and staged a scene in front of us – always pointing out to Henry what should be done. What Henry had missed. Treating him like a child. An idiot. Condescending. How – the actors should be – 'posed'.

His word. So they could be seen by all of the audience. He said this with a sort of a snicker – by now a lot of people were laughing at poor Henry. Why he stayed I have no idea.

Dorothy What could he do?

Short pause. Harley is a bit taken aback by her reaction.

Harley And then – Weston apologised – to all of us. Making a point of looking right at me. For having given someone so obviously unable or unprepared or simply untalented the responsibility for this production. He said – he alone accepted the blame. He should have known better. He should have trusted his instincts.

Sometimes, he said, he could just be – generous to a fault.

Short pause.

Henry was up there on stage with him, and he was obviously trying not to cry. I couldn't look at him.

Dorothy I told him. (*She sighs.*) I warned him. He wouldn't listen.

Pause. Music off.

Harley (*quietly*) And then it got worse.

She stares at him.

Weston said that 'unfortunately' – tongue poking cheek – there had also been a complaint by a student against Henry. He was telling the whole room this. And so he was investigating. He couldn't say more than that.

But of course he did. A minute later he was heard – talking very loudly – so everyone could hear – that was obviously intentional – talking loudly with the school Dean, about Henry being drunk at rehearsals. And even – at some classes. Do you know about this?

No response.

Henry heard this and pushed through us to defend himself. But now the Dean was saying – this was not the time or place. Henry'd have to wait. But of course the damage had been done. And then the Dean walked away.
That's it.

Hears the music.

No, one more thing – as Weston left he shouted back to everyone – 'Cap and Bells, don't forget my party!'

He listens to the music off.
Short pause.

Dorothy Was George there?

Harley Your cousin was there.

Beat.

Dorothy He's never been drunk for rehearsals.

Harley No.

Dorothy Or for any class. They made that up.

Harley (*shrugs*) A student complained.

Dorothy It was Charles Massinger.

Harley What was?

Dorothy The student who said that. About Henry.

Harley What are you talking about?

Dorothy Charles Massinger would 'complain' to Professor Weston. And then Charles would be made head of Cap and Bells.
I'm friends with the Dean's secretary. She hates all of them.

Harley Charles?

Dorothy I should have thrown you out, Mr Barker.

Harley Me? What are you talking about?

Dorothy Henry begged me to.

Harley I don't understand.

Dorothy (*upset, to herself*) Why didn't I do that?
Professor Weston has been so scared of you, Mr Barker.
You being here. Henry knew that right away. 'Tell him
to go.' 'Find him another place.'
He didn't talk to you for the whole month you've been
here, Mr Barker. Did you even notice that?

Harley Yes. Of course.

Dorothy I asked him how would Weston even know.
Oh, he'll know, he said. He'll know.

Harley Know what?

Dorothy That you were giving him ideas, Mr Barker.
For the play. 'Professional' ideas. That's what Weston
was so afraid of!

Harley That's ridiculous.

Dorothy The moment he heard you were here and he'd
already assigned the play to Henry – he started worrying.
That you were helping Henry. And this play was going
to be good. Too good. God forbid – better than his
shows. Do you understand now?

Harley But I never helped Henry . . .

Dorothy What does that matter, Mr Granville Barker?
Could Weston even tell? I doubt it. No, he'd have
attacked anything tonight.

Beatrice (*entering from the kitchen*) You're sitting in the
dark.

She has startled them. Charles is with her.

70

I didn't mean to startle you.

Harley How long have you been –?

Beatrice We came in the back. Henry came home with us. (*To Dorothy.*) He's in the kitchen. Having a drink. Don't you want more light?

Harley I think we're fine.

Beatrice It's suddenly a lovely evening outside, isn't it?

She looks at Charles in the shadows.

He was so good!

Smiles at him.
Stops, hears the distant music.

Listen to that.

Harley We were thinking it's the party Professor Weston's giving for Cap and Bells.

Beatrice (*to Charles*) That's where you're going, isn't it?

Harley He has to. He's the new President.

Charles I am . . .

Beatrice I'll be right back.

She hurries off.

Charles Where are you going? (*To the others.*) What is she doing?

He looks to them for an answer. They don't say anything. Awkward pause.

So – Mr Barker, we're all wondering what you thought?

Harley About what?

Charles (*confused, then smiles*) About the play.

Harley I enjoyed it.

Charles (*waits for more, then*) Did you like what I did? With Feste? What do you think of my prospects? To be an actor?

Harley looks at him.

Harley You seem to be a very good actor, Mr Massinger.

Charles Thank you.

He smiles at Dorothy, very pleased.

That means a lot to me. I'm such an admirer of yours.

Harley Oh, I don't think I could ever put on a performance like you did tonight.

Charles is taken aback by such praise, doesn't know what to say. Then, about the music:

Charles I'm going to have to go soon. As you said, I'm the President.

Harley Is that an elected or an appointed position?

Charles Appointed. By the faculty.

Harley Which really means – by Professor Weston.

Charles I suppose it does.

Harley You should go. Don't keep him waiting.

Beatrice returns with George. They both carry small lit candelabra.

(*To Charles.*) Look, she went to get us more light.

Beatrice I tried to get Henry to come in . . .

Charles (*to Beatrice*) Mr Barker thinks I have promise. He's been flattering me.

Beatrice (*big smile*) And so do I.

She gently touches his cheek.

You missed some . . . (*make-up*)

She stands him near the candelabra as she licks her finger and cleans the make-up, then notices the others watching.

I'll walk you to the street . . . I'll be right back.

George (*to Beatrice*) Where do you want this? (*The candlelabra.*)

Beatrice and Charles start to go towards the back door, through the kitchen. She turns back, proudly pointing to Charles.

Beatrice Feste! I have seen that play ten times and I've never even noticed the Feste before!

They go.

George I'll put it on the table.

Sets the candelabra down.

(*To Dorothy.*) Did he tell you?

Dorothy nods, as he scrapes a little wax that has fallen on the table.

(*To Dorothy.*) It wasn't fair to Henry. I wanted to stand up and shout at that man. He's just insensitive. I mean, that wasn't the time or place I thought. Of course I understand what he was trying to do. He was trying to teach the students something, but he could have been gentler. Or he could have waited.

(*To Harley.*) It wasn't very good, was it? Henry was out of his depth. I felt sorry for him. Weston made a mistake in giving him the play. And Henry suffered for it. But you never really know unless you give someone the chance, do you? So I don't really blame Weston.

Harley I enjoyed the play. I thought Henry did a very admirable job.

George You're a kind man, Mr Barker. Thank you. (*As he sits down.*) I've been asked to this party. I probably should go. I won't be long. (*Looks back to the kitchen.*) I won't go through there . . . Let him be alone. It's what I'd want . . . (*Sighs.*) I suppose I have to go. (*He stands.*) What we have to do. (*Looks at his pocket watch.*) The day never ends . . . Goodnight.

He goes off into the hallway.

Harley I'm sorry.

Dorothy George is after Henry's job. There is no opening in the English Department at this time. So there's just Henry's job. And George knows that. But he keeps coming back.

Short pause. She starts to get up, then moves about the room.

This was going to be – a lunch room. A place for the students . . . Perhaps on weekends. But they wouldn't come. That hurt me. My brother got me through that hurt.

I'm going to go sit with my brother.

The drinking, they just made that up, just in case. Just to be safe. In case it – was good tonight.

Beatrice comes back in from the kitchen.

Beatrice (*to Dorothy*) Henry said to tell you he's gone to bed.

Dorothy He just said that to get rid of you.

She goes to the kitchen.
Pause.

Beatrice Is she all right? Did you tell her about Henry?

He nods.

God, I couldn't live here . . . If I were them I'd get out of here.

Harley And do what? And go where?

Beatrice is taken aback by his vehemence.

Beatrice Did I do something . . .?

Harley (*distracted*) I'm sorry . . .

Beatrice looks off, listening to the distant music.

Beatrice He was very good, wasn't he?

Harley Who?

Beatrice Charles.

Harley Oh. Very good. You'd never know he was acting.

Beatrice turns and looks at Harley, and smiles.

Beatrice Graceful. And innocent. Wasn't he innocent? With that beautiful cherub face. That worked for Feste. I wasn't sure it would. Feste's a little . . .

She looks for the word.

Harley Devious?

Beatrice I suppose.

Harley Duplicitous?

Beatrice But it did work. You have to admit that. I think he has a real career in the theatre. Don't you?

Harley It's a difficult business. It can crush people.

Beatrice I know that. He knows that – at least in theory. He hasn't experienced . . . As we have. But if it is something he wants . . . Very badly. And if he doesn't lose that – passion. He has – passion. He has that now . . .

Harley And no, you don't want to lose that.

She looks at him, confused.

Beatrice Passion?

No response.
She looks out of the window.

There's something special about American acting, isn't there? It's earthy. Less guarded. Don't you think? Those boys tonight . . .

Harley Are they really actors?

Beatrice I disagree, Harley. What do you mean?

Harley In the sense that you and I mean it. 'Actors'. The theatre.

Beatrice They may not be adequately trained . . . yet. But still I thought it was beautiful. My heart was in my throat for more than two hours.

Harley Good.

Beatrice (*smiles*) Even when Feste wasn't on stage. So it wasn't just that.

Harley Good.

Beatrice Feste isn't on stage that much . . .
I'm thinking of asking my husband for a divorce too.

Harley 'Too'? You mean like –?

Beatrice Like you. What's the matter?
Charles and I talked about it.

Harley Does he know anything? Your husband?

Beatrice No.

Harley Sleep on it. For a few weeks. And calm down.

Beatrice My husband thinks I'm giving a lecture this weekend.

Harley So let him think that.

Beatrice I have three children, Harley. What should I do?

No response.

I hate it when Charles talks about the war. I'm hoping his father can do something about that. Knock some sense into him. Pull some strings. And I get worried that – the world of the theatre, it could . . . You know. You know what it's like. I like him as he is now.

Harley I know what it's like.

Beatrice So what do you think I should do?

No response.
  Short pause. The music.

Oh, I'd love to be there. At this party. I should be there. Some of the other boys were bringing their girls. I saw that. So there are girls there. Why can't I go?

Harley Beatrice.

She looks at him.

Charles . . .

Beatrice Charles – what? He's what?

Harley Nothing. I mean – he was a good Feste.

Beatrice I know. (*She smiles and looks off.*) So what should I do? What would you do? How did you explain it to your wife?

Short pause.

Harley I don't think I have.

Beatrice What? You said –

Harley (*upset*) Or maybe I just didn't say the right things! I don't know! And I don't know what you should do! So please stop asking me!

They are both taken aback by his outburst. Then:

I don't know. I don't know. (*He looks at her.*) Trust me, you do not want advice about this from me. (*He looks at her.*) Lillah's answer . . . (*Hands it to Beatrice.*) She says – no.

Beatrice reads the letter.

Beatrice Harley . . .

Short pause.

Harley Everything I do, I feel like I'm waiting for it – whatever it is – to be over. I – I have breakfast, I wait for that to be over. I go for a walk – when is that going to be over? It doesn't take long, until . . . when is it all over?

He looks up at her.

But thank God I can use it too. I tell myself – you still have an article to finish. So wait until that's over. You still have a book you're reading. Wait for that . . . So . . .

He has taken out of his pocket a pile of letters and hands them to her.

Here . . . letters from friends.

Beatrice You haven't even opened all of them.

Harley I know what they say. They blame me. Lillah has worked hard at that.

Beatrice What about the new woman?

Harley Perhaps. She's waiting too.

Beatrice Good. Tell me about her.

No response.

Or don't.

> *She looks at a letter. She reads it, turns it over, finishes it.*
> *Pause.*
> *Beatrice stands, offers the letters back to Harley. He*
> *doesn't take them. She sets them down and picks up*
> *one of the candelabra to take upstairs. She stops.*

That was so cruel what that professor did to poor
Henry. When we were walking back here – I was so
proud of Charles. He kept telling Henry how much he
liked his direction. How good a director he thought
Henry was. Charles didn't have to do that. Most young
people wouldn't even think of doing that.
  I am sorry about your wife.

> *She reaches and takes his hand and holds it.*

What am I going to do?

Harley That should be my line. That's what I should say.

> *They smile.*

(*Holding her hand.*) You know, I think this is the first
time in over a month that I have touched another human
being . . .

> *She leaves with the candelabra. After a moment,*
> *Harley blows out the remaining candles and sits in the*
> *dark.*
> *Distant music.*

End of Scene Four.

SCENE FIVE

The backyard of the boarding house. The same as Scene One.

An afternoon in late May. Brilliant sunshine. Frank is being brought outside by Dorothy. Frank now wears a black armband.

Dorothy How long do you plan on wearing that? (*The armband.*)

Frank *You're* asking me that?

She smiles.

Dorothy I know.

Frank (*hesitates, then*) I don't know how long. Maybe another few weeks. I'll know when . . . . Where is everyone? Mr Barker invited me to lunch.

Dorothy Lunch will be part of it.

Frank Part of what?

Harley enters. He carries a long white jacket – a costume – over his arm, and a white doctor's hat.

Harley Frank! (*As they greet, to Dorothy.*) Was the train late?

Dorothy I don't know. He just arrived.

Frank (*explaining his lateness*) I walked from the station. Such a beautiful day.

Harley (*over this*) You made it!

Frank What's going on?

Others now come from the house, all in costumes: Henry in a long coat and a fake white beard; George as a Turkish Knight; Charles as St George with his horse around his waist; Beatrice as a valiant British soldier.

What is this? Why are you dressed like that? Henry. Mrs Hale –

Beatrice We were just doing one of Henry's Italian rehearsals in the dining room.

Frank George –

George My mouth's limber.

Frank A Mummers' play? Why?

Harley When we heard you were going to do *A Tale of Two Cities* in Pittsfield – we had the idea of doing this for you.

Beatrice Harley telegrammed . . .

Harley Beatrice came up last night.

Beatrice I am always looking for any excuse.

She playfully rubs Charles's back.

Frank (*greeting*) Charles. Who made you St George?

Charles Mr Spraight.

Beatrice I did! I'm the valiant knight!

Henry Charles found some costumes – and says he didn't tell Professor Weston.

Charles I'm the President of Cap and Bells.

Harley A position well earned.

Henry My sister made the rest.

Dorothy I've volunteered ten times to sew costumes for their shows. They never want me.

Henry And George is here every weekend anyway.

Frank Are you, George?

Dorothy Where do we sit? (*To Frank.*) We're the audience. You and me.

Harley So you're not looking into the sun. Over there.

Henry I have the chairs.

Beatrice (*over this to Charles*) Help him.

Chairs are moved. (Note: the performance of the Mummers' play should not be directed out to the audience. It should feel like a private, intimate event, done only for themselves.)

Frank I can't believe you're doing this. So, Harley, this is what you're producing now? (*Smiles.*)

Harley No. No. One time. One time only.

Beatrice (*to Frank*) How was the funeral?

This gets everyone's attention.
  Frank looks at them all.

Frank She had friends. I was moved by that. Mostly from the church. I hadn't realised she'd spent that much time at the church. So – there was a bit of a crowd at the cemetery. She would have liked that.

Harley Where is the cemetery?

Frank Brooklyn.
  I know – far away. I was the only English person there. I don't know what that means.

Short pause.

Beatrice Harley, before we begin, tell Frank what you were just talking about inside.

Henry He's writing a book.

Harley Starting one. Let's just do the –

Henry About theatre.

Beatrice Tell him, Harley. It's fascinating.

Harley (*to Frank*) It has nothing to do with Dickens.

Beatrice Tell him.

The others look to him, then:

Harley (*to Frank*) I . . . I decided that – it does matter. The theatre. Or could matter. But that – even though it may seem sometimes like a waste of time – or worse – it can't go away.

And no matter how it gets distorted – mangled and used by others who don't understand – it comes back. Always, because – and I remembered I used to tell my actors this when we started staging – I haven't for years, I'd forgotten about it. But I would tell them – that the theatre, it is the only artistic form that uses the entire live human being as its expression.

Nothing between them – and us. Just like this.

Gestures between himself and the others.

You and me. Talking, and listening. Intimacy. And as long as we have this (*us*) – theatre will find its way or its way back. Because – when we no longer have this (*us*) – it'll mean, we're dead.

Short pause.

Dorothy Which we're not.

Others look at Dorothy, then:

Harley Let's do this play . . . And Frank – I'm not saying this is what theatre should be.

Beatrice Listen to him!

Harley I'm serious. I think I'm just – looking for something. *Beginning* to look. For something I think I lost.

> *The others move out of the way – creating a space for the 'stage'. All will stand and watch the others, and react.*

(*To Frank*) Henry found different versions in the college's library.

Henry I liked this one.

Harley It doesn't have a dragon . . . (*To the others.*) Move back. Move. Henry . . . (*To Frank.*) We begin.

> *Frank and Dorothy are the audience.*

Frank (*to Dorothy*) 'A Mummers' Play'. In America. In the summertime.

> *Henry 'enters' as Father Christmas. He walks around swinging his club, clearing the room.*

Henry
'Here come I old Father Christmas,
Welcome or welcome not,
I hope old Father Christmas
Will never be forgot –

Although it's Father Christmas
I've a short time to stay,
But I've come to show you pleasure
Before I pass away!'

> *Reaction from the others: 'Ohhh . . .' because he is going to die.*

'Make room, make room, my gallants, room,
And give us space to rhyme;

We've come to show St George's play
Upon this Christmas time.'

Beatrice, the Valiant Knight, 'enters' with her sword.

Beatrice
'Here come I the Valiant Soldier,
Slasher is my name –'

Others react in mock horror.

(*To them.*) Thank you.

'With sword and buckler by my side,
I hope to win the game.
One of my brethren I've seen wownded,
Another I've seen slain,
So I will fight with any foe
Upon this British plain.'

Dorothy (*to Frank*) Or Williamstown.

George, the Turkish Knight, 'enters' with his sword.

George
'Here come I, the Turkish Knight,
Come from the Turkish land to fight;
I'll fight St George and all his crew,
Aye, countryfolk and warriors too.'

Beatrice/Valiant Knight steps forward.

Beatrice
'If thou art called the Turkish Knight,
Draw out thy sword, and let us fight!
I am a friend of good St George,
I've fought men o'er and o'er,
And for the sake of good St George
I'd fight a hundred more.'

*They fight and there is much ohhhhing and ahhhhing
by the others. Beatrice falls down 'dying'.*

'To slay this false knight did I try –
'Tis for the right to have to die!'

She 'dies'.
 George as Turkish Knight marches around.

George
'If St George but meet me here
I'll try his mettle without fear.'

*As the play continues, the projections on page 84
begin.*
 *Charles enters as St George. He hurries on, excited.
He is not a good actor.*

Charles
'Here come I, St George, the valiant man,
With glittering sword and spear in hand!
So haste away, make no delay,
For I can give some lusty lumps,
And, like a true born Englishman,
Fight on my legs or on my stumps!'

Frank (*to everyone*) My wife would have loved this . . .

The others hear this, are moved, but keep going.
 George as Turkish Knight advances.

George
'Make not so bold, St George, I pray;
Though thou'rt all this, thou'rt one I'll slay!'

*They fight, more crowd reactions. George is
'wounded' and falls on one knee.*

Charles
'Can there a doctor come to me
From anywhere in this countree?'

Henry as Father Christmas looks around.

Henry

'Is there a doctor to be found
To cure this man of his deadly wownd?
For whatsoever wrath you feel
Towards your foeman, we must heal.'

*Harley has put on his Doctor's costume and now
enters.*

Harley

'Yes, there's a doctor to be found
To cure this man of his deadly wownd.
With this small bottle –

Takes out a bottle.

That you see
I cure all evils there can be;
The phthisic, the palsy and the gout,
If the devil's in I'll blow him out.'

Henry

'Doctor then, O what's thy fee,
For doing of this great mercee?'

Harley

'Fifty pound is my fee –

Others react.

But ten pounds less I'll take of thee.'

Henry

'What does say, he? Half a crown?'

Harley

'No, I tell thee forty poun' –
A small sum that to save a man,
And you've the money in your han'.

*He takes the money. (The projections end here.)
    Harley as Doctor speaks to the 'audience' – the
others directly.*

87

Being a doctor of great fame
Who from the ancient countries came,
And knowing Asia, Afric-ay,
And every mystery out that way,
I've learned to do the best of cures
For all the human frame endures.
I can restore a leg or arm
From mortification or more harm,
I can repair a sword-slit pate,
A leg cut off – if not too late.'

End of play.

Projections during the Mummers' Play

TWO YEARS LATER LILLAH
GRANTED HARLEY A DIVORCE

HE AND HELEN MARRIED THE SAME YEAR

HELEN'S HUSBAND MADE HER A SURPRISINGLY
GENEROUS SETTLEMENT

HARLEY ABANDONED THE PROFESSIONAL THEATRE
AND AVOIDED ACADEME

BECAME THE FIRST CHAIRMAN OF A NATIONAL
ORGANISATION OF AMATEUR THEATRES IN THE UK

WROTE PREFACES TO IMAGINED PRODUCTIONS OF
SHAKESPEARE PLAYS

AND A BOOK ABOUT AN EXEMPLARY THEATRE

Author's Note

This play is inspired by fact. Harley Granville Barker did write to his wife, Lillah McCarthy, in January 1916, asking for a divorce so he could marry the American, Helen Huntington. In February 1916, Barker left France where he was researching his book on the Red Cross, and returned to London to meet with Lillah, hoping to get a positive decision. This was the last time they would ever meet. Barker then left for America where he settled in Williamstown, Massachusetts, for several months – staying, not in a boarding house, but the much larger Williams Inn.

While in Williamstown, besides letters Barker wrote the one-act play *Farewell to the Theatre*, began the book *An Exemplary Theatre* and probably started work on what would become the play *The Secret Life*. In this play, Barker sets a climactic scene (III, ii) in a little sitting room in 'Countesbury, Massachusetts', clearly a stand-in for Williamstown.

We also know that while in Williamstown Barker lectured throughout New England. There are records of his lectures at Mt Holyoke College (as well as his attending an all-girl *Twelfth Night* there) and Wellesley College. And at Williams College, we know he attended at least one 'Smoker' and was resident there during the Cap and Bells Production of *Twelfth Night*, with Charles Massinger, recently promoted to head of this society, playing Feste. Etc., etc.

Frank Spraight was the 'Dickens' man (the clipping Harley reads in the play is indeed from the *New York Times*), who had the same lecture agent as did Barker (J. B. Pond, with offices in the Metropolitan Life Building, etc.), though there is no evidence of Frank being in Williamstown at this time, nor of his knowing Barker. Beatrice too is based on a real character, the niece of Forbes-Robertson; she was an actress, lecturer (with Feakins), and we know that her marriage to an American lawyer was in trouble at this time (she had recently discovered letters by him to 'Evelyn', a painter he was 'nurturing'). Again, there is no evidence that she was in Williamstown at this time, nor that she had a relationship with Charles Massinger.

There was also a 'George' who gave the talk discussed in the play and who followed Barker at various colleges during the 'tercentenary' celebration of Shakespeare.

At the time of the play, Barker was indeed broke, and he and Helen Huntington expected little help from Helen's rich husband. A teaching position could easily have seemed, for a moment, tempting to him. He seems, at this time, to have been looking for something, and at a loss about what that was or could be.

In the scene in *The Secret Life* mentioned above, set in a very Williamstown-like setting, Barker has Joan ask Mr Kittredge: 'What held you in place?' (By which she means: what kept you from killing yourself?) And he answers: 'Inconsequent things. Once, it was the thought of an unfinished book that had been paid for. Once, a night's sleep made all the difference . . .'

Then she asks: 'Did the troubles pass?' 'No,' he answers. 'They were unsolved problems. I face them still.'

I have used the facts to inspire a play.

In researching *Farewell to the Theatre*, I consulted numerous books, newspapers, etc. I mention only the most important – three biographies/critical studies of Barker: C. B. Purdom's *Harley Granville Barker*, Dennis

Kennedy's *Granville Barker and the Dream of Theatre* and, most importantly, Eric Salmon's ground-breaking study, *Granville Barker: A Secret Life*; Michael Holroyd's masterpiece, the four-volume *Bernard Shaw*; Lillah McCarthy's *Myself and My Friends*; Mander and Mitchenson's *Theatrical Companion to Shaw*; Edward Gordon Craig's *The Theatre Advancing*; Janet Leeper's *Edward Gordon Craig*; Ian Clarke's *Edwardian Drama*; and Colin Wilson's *The Outsider*.

I have read and re-read, pillaged from and been inspired by all the works of Harley Granville Barker. I have 'borrowed' from *The Exemplary Theatre, The Secret Life* and his essay, 'The Heritage of the Actor', which he wrote as an introduction to *The Secret Life* but which was published separately; and, as already mentioned, from his collected letters. I have also found useful a series of interviews with Barker published in the *New York Times* in 1915 and 1916. And of course I stole one of his play titles.

I am also in debt to *The Williams Record*, the Williams College Newspaper. I possess copies of every edition published between March and June 1916. And many of the details of the play were discovered here.

And finally, from the many possible Mummers' plays, I chose the one that Thomas Hardy describes in *The Return of the Native*, and then privately published. Barker knew Hardy well (having directed his *The Dynasts* in London); and later, when the Granville Barkers moved to Devon, the Hardys were frequent guests. Even though this version was not published in 1916, I chose it for this reason, and because of the Doctor's speech.

Richard Nelson
Rhinebeck, New York